# contents

# Introduction
## *Brenda Kitchen*

The inspiration for my book comes from almost 20 years of creating recipes for 'Simply Cooking' and from my wonderful nan!

'Simply Cooking' is the name of my fresh food company. My loyal sponsors have supported my idea that simple, home-cooked food has widespread appeal.

For as long as I can remember, food has meant more to me than merely a way to satisfy hunger. Food is my life passion. In this book, you will discover recipes that are fast and fabulous, plus slow, tasty winter warmers such as Brenda's Irish stew. With comfort in mind, this book is a mixture of fast and slow offerings.

I hope you enjoy cooking my recipes, and may the aromas of real comfort food fill your kitchen and delight you as they do me.

4

*Cooking with feeling ~ Brenda*

*Quick & Easy*

# Comfort
# Food

igloo

igloo

This edition published in 2009
by Igloo Books Ltd
Cottage Farm
Sywell
NN6 OBJ
www.igloo-books.com

© R&R Publications,
Anthony Carroll, 2007

10 9 8 7 6 5 4 3 2 1

ISBN: 978 1 84817 459 7

Printed and manufactured in China

**Disclaimer:** The nutritional information listed with each recipe is calculated on a per serve basis and does not include the nutrient content of garnishes or any accompaniments not listed in specific quantities in the ingredient list. The nutritional information for each recipe is an estimate only, and may vary depending on the brand of ingredients used, and due to natural biological variations in the composition of natural foods such as meat, fish, fruit and vegetables. The nutritional information was calculated by using the computer program Foodworks dietary analysis software (version 4, Xyris Software Pty. Ltd. Queensland Australia), and is based on the Australian food composition tables and food manufacturers' data. Where not specified, ingredients are always analysed as average or medium, not small or large.

# A warm and *wonderful world*

My nan played a part inspiring me to write this book. She created for me a warm and wonderful world in which food played a huge role.

My brother Brian and I lived with Nan and Pa from when we were very young. We were raised in Clovelly, a seaside suburb of Sydney, Australia. The beach was a short stroll down the steep hill of Melrose Parade, and I have fond memories of long summer days spent at the beach with my friends and returning home to good old-fashioned meals. I remember that Nan always cooked the best roast dinners for Sunday lunch. There's nothing like the smell and taste of a roast dinner after spending a morning at the beach – days of true comfort!

The Sunday roast consisted mainly of lamb with crispy baked potatoes, pumpkin, fresh beans and, of course, lots of gravy. It was always a home-made gravy, not the bought stuff some like to call gravy. Gravy really completes a roast dinner, and it's so easy to make with some simple ingredients and a little patience. Combining 20-minute meals with some old-fashioned home cooking is a perfect way to balance your time in the kitchen.

*Food has always inspired my imagination*

# Magic
## *healing foods*

**These foods have healing powers. Eat lots of them!**

| | |
|---|---|
| **Bananas** | are an excellent source of potassium. |
| **Broccoli** | is an excellent source of calcium and assists calcium absorption. |
| **Cabbage** | is known to have cancer-fighting properties. |
| **Garlic** | is nature's antibiotic. It's an energy-booster for the immune system. |
| **Potatoes** | are a fantastic source of fiber. |
| **Pumpkin** | contains betacarotene, an excellent antioxidant. |
| **Olive oil** | moisturizes the skin and is healthy to cook with. |
| **Onions** | purify the blood. |
| **Spinach** | is a rich source of iron and is high in vitamins and minerals. |
| **Tomatoes** | are a rich source of antioxidants. |

**Fat** is needed in your diet. A little fat provides flavor and long-lasting satisfaction, which prevents the need to snack in between meals.

*Have a creative time in the kitchen and relax by preparing early, so you can really enjoy your tasty meal*

# *marvelous*
# *meats*

# marvelous meats

**Hint:** Irish stew is delicious, but you must use the best neck lamb chops. I'm not sure why their flavor is so very different from other lamb chops, but I have found that if you don't use neck chops, you don't get the same flavor. If you want to make your stew extra creamy, add a little milk to the dish.

**Hint:** Usually chili con carne has red kidney beans but I've chosen to use the three bean mix. It gives the dish a lovely flavor and different look and texture. It really tastes fantastic!

## brenda's *irish stew*

### INGREDIENTS

**8 best neck lamb chops**
**3 large old potatoes, peeled and sliced thickly**
**2 large carrots, sliced**
**½ cup fresh parsley, chopped**
**salt and pepper to taste**
**2 tablespoons plain flour**
**a little milk, optional**

**Serves** 4 **Calories** 425
**Fat** 8.2 **Preparation** 10 mins
**Cooking** 1 hr 40 mins

### METHOD

**1** Preheat the oven to 356°F/180°C. Layer th chops, potatoes, carrots and parsley in a casserole dish. Season to taste and cover with boiling water. Put the lid on the casserole and cook in the oven for 1½ hours.

**2** Thicken by mixing the plain flour with a little sauce from the stew. Stir into the stew and place back into the oven for a further 10 minutes. For a creamy gravy, replace some of the liquid from the stew with a little milk after cooking.

## chili *con carne*

### INGREDIENTS

**1 onion, finely chopped**
**1 clove garlic, crushed**
**1 tablespoon olive oil**
**1 lb/500g extra-lean beef mince**
**1 lb/500g medium-hot tomato salsa**
**15 oz/425g canned three bean mix, drained**
**1 bay leaf**
**1 green capsicum, finely chopped**
**½ cup beef stock**
**salt and pepper to taste**

### METHOD

**1** Gently fry the onion and garlic in the olive oil until softened. Add the mince and cook until it changes color.

**2** Add the remaining ingredients and simmer for 40 minutes. Serve with corn chips, grated cheese, sour cream and guacamole.

**Variation:** Create nachos by lining a baking dish with corn chips and topping with chili con carne and grated cheese. Bake at 356°F/180°C for 20 minutes.

**Serves** 4 **Calories** 511 **Fat** 7.5 **Preparation** 10 mins **Cooking** 45 mins

chili con carne

9

# pasta bake

# pasta bake

## INGREDIENTS

1 large onion, chopped

1 clove garlic, crushed

5⅓ oz/150g lean bacon, chopped

3 large mushrooms, chopped

1 teaspoon ground paprika

1 teaspoon oregano leaves

1 tablespoon olive oil

1 lb/500g lean beef mince

10⅔ oz/300g tomato salsa

½ red capsicum, chopped

1 cup basil leaves, chopped

2 bay leaves

1 lb/500g spaghetti, cooked
and drained

1 lb/500g Cheddar cheese, grated

**topping**

3 oz/80g Cheddar cheese, grated

2 eggs, beaten

1 cup fresh breadcrumbs, toasted

## METHOD

**1** Preheat the oven to 356°F/180°C. Fry the onion, garlic, bacon, mushrooms, paprika and oregano in the olive oil until softened.

**2** Add the beef mince and cook over a high heat until it changes color and breaks into small pieces.

**3** Add the salsa, capsicum, basil and bay leaves. Simmer for 30 minutes.

**4** Layer the spaghetti with the meat sauce and cheese into a large, shallow baking dish.

**5** To make the topping, combine the cheese with the eggs. Pour over the top of the spaghetti bake, then sprinkle with the breadcrumbs.

**6** Bake for 30 minutes until golden brown. Serve with a crisp green salad.

**Hint:** Any variety of salsa or flavored Italian-style tomato sauces can be used to make a good pasta bake. Keep your eye out for new varieties on the supermarket shelf.

11

**Serves** 6 **Calories** 611 **Fat** 9.7 **Preparation** 10 mins **Cooking** 1 hr 10 mins

# marvelous meats

**Hint:** Serve with creamy mashed potato and a green vegetable. This also makes a wonderful winter pie with some pre-made shortcrust pastry.

**Hint:** If you like spicy pepper steak, then use a generous amount of seasoned pepper or pepper steak seasoning. Make sure to use a tender cut of meat, such as rump steak, T-bone or sirloin.

## hearty stew

### INGREDIENTS

2.2 lb/1kg stewing steak, cubed

2 tablespoons plain flour

2 teaspoons sugar

3 onions, sliced

1 teaspoon crushed garlic

7 oz/200g lean bacon, finely chopped

1 tablespoon olive oil

1 tablespoon worcestershire sauce

2 tablespoons malt vinegar

10⅔ oz/300g tomato salsa

sea salt

cracked black peppercorns

**Serves** 6 **Calories** 328

**Fat** 4.7g **Preparation** 10 mins

**Cooking** 2 hrs 10 mins

### METHOD

**1** Coat the stewing steak in flour and sugar and set aside.

**2** In a large heavy-based frying pan, fry the onions, garlic and bacon in the olive oil until softened. Add the stewing steak and cook for a few minutes to seal in the flavor.

**3** Add the rest of the ingredients, season to taste and simmer for 2 hours.

## creamy pepper steak

### INGREDIENTS

1 tablespoon butter

1 lb/500g rump steak, trimmed

sprinkle of black pepper

¼ red parsley and chives, chopped

3 tablespoons cream

salt and pepper to taste

**Serves** 2 **Calories** 108.5

**Fat** 3.4g **Preparation** 5 mins

**Cooking** 10 mins

### METHOD

**1** Melt the butter in a frying pan and add the rump steak and lightly sprinkle with pepper. Cook until lightly browned, then turn and lightly sprinkle the other side with the pepper.

**2** Before the rump steak is cooked, add the parsley and chives. Then add the cream. If you want a lot of sauce, add all the cream. If only a little sauce is required, add only 1 or 2 tablespoons of cream.

**3** Turn the rump steak several times in the sauce, season to taste, then serve.

creamy pepper steak

# basic pie filling

# basic pie filling

### INGREDIENTS

1lb/500g lean beef mince

1 medium onion, finely chopped

salt and pepper to taste

1 teaspoon mixed herbs

1 cup water

2 tablespoons plain flour, mixed to a paste with water

### METHOD

**1** Place the mince, half the onion, salt and pepper, mixed herbs and water into a saucepan and bring to the boil.

**2** Reduce the heat to a simmer, cover the saucepan and cook for 30 minutes.

**3** Add the rest of the onion and the flour mixture to the mince a little at a time until thickened. Adjust seasonings if necessary.

**Serves** 4 **Calories** 288 **Fat** 8g **Preparation** 30 mins **Cooking** 35 mins

**Hint:** You can add alternative vegetables of your choice to this recipe, such as peas or beans.

# meat and potato pie

If you've not got much time, you can try this cheat's version. It's really easy and saves hours of cooking time.

### INGREDIENTS

1 medium onion, finely chopped

2 tablespoons of cooking oil

2 carrots, peeled and sliced

2 medium potatpes, peeled and thickly sliced

1 can of stewed steak in gravy

1 pack of ready-made shortcrust pastry

A little milk to glaze

### METHOD

**1** Preheat the oven to 437°F/225°C. Fry the onions in the oil until soft. Leave to cool. Boil the carrots for 10 minutes, or until cooked to taste. Boil the potatoes for 10 minutes. Leave the vegetables to cool.

**2** Empty the can of steak into a non-stick pie dish. Mix the cooled onions, carrots and potatoes in with the steak. Place the pre-made shortcrust pastry on top of the pie filling and cut aroud the edge. Pinch the edges of the pastry to seal and glaze with milk.

**3** Bake in the oven for 30-35 minutes or until the pastry is browned.

**Serves** 4

**Preparation** 10 mins

**Cooking** 35 mins

15

**Hint:** This is a very simple dish, yet it tastes fantastic and is a healthy and casual meal.

**Serves** 4 **Calories** 210
**Fat** 2.3g **Preparation** 10 mins
**Cooking** 10 mins

# moroccan lamb salad wraps

## INGREDIENTS

1 lb/500g lean lamb
sprinkle of Moroccan-style seasoning
1 tablespoon olive oil
mixed salad leaves
a few chopped mint leaves
3 tomatoes, sliced
cucumber, thinly sliced
1 medium red onion, sliced
1 red capsicum, thinly sliced
juice of 2 lemons
1 tablespoon olive oil
Tortilla wraps

## METHOD

**1** Sprinkle the sliced lamb with Moroccan seasoning and fry in the olive oil for a few minutes, but don't overcook.

**2** Combine the lamb with all the remaining ingredients except the wraps.

**3** Put a generous amount of the lamb and salad mixture into the tortilla wraps and serve immediately.

# mini meaty balls

## INGREDIENTS

1⅔ lb/750g lean mince
½ in/1cm piece ginger, freshly chopped
1 bunch fresh chives, chopped
½ bunch fresh coriander, chopped
1 egg
sprinkle of garlic steak seasoning
dry breadcrumbs, to coat

## METHOD

**1** Preheat a large frying pan. Mix all the ingredients except the breadcrumbs in a bowl. Using a dessertspoon, form small balls. Coat the meaty balls with the dry breadcrumbs.

**2** Dry-fry the meaty balls for 8–10 minutes, turning every couple of minutes.

**Hint:** This is a lovely recipe if you want to serve mini cocktail meaty balls before dinner. With a few basic ingredients, including the mince, fresh ginger and fresh coriander, you're giving your mini meaty balls lots of flavor. Next time you're having a party, serve some mini meaty balls each on toothpicks.

**Serves** 6 **Calories** 353
**Fat** 9.1g **Preparation** 10 mins
**Cooking** 10 mins

17

# supreme bolognese

**Serves** 4  **Calories** 98

**Fat** 0.7g  **Preparation** 10 mins

**Cooking** 40 mins

## INGREDIENTS

1 tablespoon olive oil

1 large brown onion, finely chopped

2 cloves garlic, crushed

2½ oz/70g lean bacon, chopped

1 lb/500g extra-lean beef mince

1 teaspoon ground paprika

pinch of sugar

14 oz/400g canned whole tomatoes

2 tablespoons tomato paste

7 oz/200g mushrooms, chopped

½ cup fresh basil, chopped

¼ teaspoon chili flakes

½ cup red wine

½ teaspoon sea salt

½ teaspoon cracked black peppercorns

## METHOD

**1** Heat a frying pan. Add the olive oil, onion, garlic and bacon and cook until softened. Add the mince and cook until it changes color, breaking the mince up with a fork as you are cooking.

**2** Add all the remaining ingredients and simmer until cooked, for about 30 minutes. Serve with freshly cooked spaghetti.

# rich and tasty pork chops

## INGREDIENTS

2 teaspoons olive oil

4 large pork chops

1 large onion, chopped

2 cloves garlic, crushed

1 stalk chopped celery

½ red capsicum, chopped

3 small eggplants, sliced

10⅔ oz/300g tomato salsa

12 black olives

## METHOD

**1** Heat the oil in a frying pan and brown the pork chops.

**2** Remove the chops, add all the vegetables and cook until soft.

**3** Add the chops, salsa and olives to the pan. Simmer on a very low heat for 1 hour. Serve with creamy mashed potato and pumpkin and a fresh green vegetable.

**Hint:** Lean pork cuts can be used in this recipe.

**Serves** 4 **Calories** 385

**Fat** 4.3g **Preparation** 10 mins

**Cooking** 1 hr 10 mins

19

**Hint:** You can substitute any topping of your choice.

**Serves** 2  **Calories** 87
**Fat** 2.8g  **Preparation** 5 mins
**Cooking** 15 mins

# meat lover's pizza

## INGREDIENTS

½ lb/250g lean beef mince
2 tablespons cooking oil
sprinkle of seasoned pepper
salt to taste
2 tablespoons tomato salsa
2 oz/50g Cheddar cheese, grated
sprinkle of chives, chopped
sprinkle of fresh parsley, chopped
sprinkle of ground paprika

## METHOD

**1** Heat oil in a frying pan. Press the mince onto the bottom of the pan to form the base of the 'pizza'. Sprinkle with seasoned pepper and salt to taste. Cook, covered, on high until the mince changes color. Turn the meat and continue to cook for a few minutes.

**2** Place the salsa, cheese, chopped chives, parsley and paprika onto the mince and cook on medium, covered, for 5–7 minutes or until the cheese melts. Serve with vegetables as a main meal or with salad and crusty bread as a snack.

# tasty
## chicken

**Hint:** Where possible, buy your chicken free-range or corn-fed for beautiful tasting birds. You will notice the extra flavor and character of this delicately flavored poultry.

# chicken parmigiana

### INGREDIENTS

2 teaspoons olive oil

1 lb/500g crumbed chicken schnitzel

10²/₃ oz/300g tomato salsa

3 oz/80g low-fat cheese, grated

sprinkle of ground paprika

sprinkle of fresh parsley, chopped

sprinkle of fresh chives, chopped

**Serves** 4  **Calories** 369

**Fat** 2.3g  **Preparation** 5 mins

**Cooking** 10 mins

### METHOD

**1** Heat the oil in a frying pan. Cook the schnitzel on high until lightly browned. Turn and spread some of the salsa on the schnitzel until covered. Sprinkle the cheese on top.

**2** Sprinkle the schnitzel with paprika, parsley and chives.
Cover the frying pan until the cheese has melted, then serve with potato wedges and green beans.

# curried chicken

### INGREDIENTS

1 large onion, chopped

1 carrot, chopped

1 stalk celery, chopped

2 teaspoons butter

mild curry powder to taste

8 chicken drumsticks, skin removed

1–1½ cups hot water

salt and pepper to taste

½–¾ cup low-fat milk

sprinkle of fresh parsley, chopped

2 tablespoons plain flour, mixed to a paste with milk

### METHOD

**1** In a large frying pan, soften the vegetables in the butter, add curry powder to taste and cook for 30 seconds. Add the chicken, water and salt and pepper to taste, and simmer on a low heat for 40 minutes or until the chicken is tender.

**2** Drain off some of the liquid and replace it with the low-fat milk. Bring back to a simmer, add the parsley and thicken with the flour mixture, adding it slowly and stirring until the sauce is the desired consistency. Serve with boiled rice.

**Serves** 4  **Calories** 460  **Fat** 8.9g

**Preparation** 10 mins  **Cooking** 50 mins

curried chicken

# easy crumbed chicken

# easy crumbed chicken

## INGREDIENTS

1 lb/500g chicken breast fillet

sprinkle of lemon pepper
seasoning

1 tablespoon plain flour

1 egg

½ cup dry breadcrumbs

2 tablespoons olive oil

salt to taste

juice of 1 lemon

sprinkle of fresh chives, chopped

sprinkle of fresh parsley,
chopped

Serves 4  Calories 316

Fat 2g  Preparation 5 mins

Cooking 10 mins

## METHOD

**1** Slice the chicken breast thinly and place in a plastic bag. Sprinkle with lemon pepper seasoning. Seal the bag and shake gently until the lemon pepper seasoning is spread evenly over the chicken.

**2** Add the flour to coat the chicken and shake in the bag until it is evenly coated. Break the egg into the bag and hold the top securely as you massage the egg into the other ingredients. Now add the breadcrumbs, and once again seal the bag and shake until the chicken is coated.

**3** Heat oil in a frying pan. Add the crumbed chicken and cook until it browns. Add salt to taste, turn the chicken and squeeze on some lemon juice. Add the fresh chopped chives and parsley, then cover and cook for approximately 3 minutes.

## baking crumbed food

Like most children, my boys loved crispy crumbed drumsticks, golden and crunchy on the outside, tender and moist on the inside.

I've never been a big fan of high-fat food and over the years I've developed some easy alternative cooking methods.

This baking method works well for most crumbed foods, such as chicken pieces, veal or lamb, salmon rissoles and crumbed meatloaf.

Nan made her own breadcrumbs by putting any leftover bread on baking trays. These were placed in the oven to dry out in the stored heat left over from cooking the evening meal. Nothing was wasted in Nan's kitchen, not even odd bits of bread!

**Hint:** Why not make gourmet breadcrumbs by adding a few simple ingredients to store-bought breadcrumbs? Experiment with the following: ground paprika, chopped chives, freshly grated Parmesan cheese, mixed herbs, rosemary, oregano or parsley, chili flakes and garlic salt, lemon pepper seasoning or lemongrass and chili. A super breadcrumb topping is equal parts of grated Cheddar cheese and breadcrumbs, with freshly chopped chives, paprika and chili flakes.

# easy chicken stir-fry

### INGREDIENTS

10⅔ oz/300g chicken breast fillets

1 tablespoon sweet chili sauce

1 tablespoon hoisin sauce

1 tablespoon soy sauce

½ teaspoon chili flakes

1 red capsicum, diced

1 green capsicum, diced

6 shallots, diced

1 head broccoli, separated into florets

### METHOD

**1** Thinly slice the chicken breast fillets. Heat a frying pan, add the sweet chili sauce, hoisin sauce, soy sauce and chili flakes and stir well.

**2** When the sauce begins to bubble, add the chicken fillets and stir to combine. Cook for 2 minutes, then add the vegetables and stir-fry. Cover and cook for another 3 minutes, stirring regularly. Serve with boiled rice.

**Serves** 4  **Calories** 68

**Fat** 0.1g  **Preparation** 5 mins

**Cooking** 10 mins

# creamy mustard chicken

### INGREDIENTS

2 teaspoons olive oil

2 teaspoons butter

1 lb/500g chicken breast fillets

sprinkle of lemon pepper seasoning

2 tablespoons plain flour

2 teaspoons German mustard

2 tablespoons cream

sprinkle of fresh parsley, chopped

### METHOD

**1** Heat the butter and olive oil on medium heat in a frying pan. Coat the chicken in lemon pepper seasoning and plain flour and add to pan. You can cook the chicken in strips or as whole breast fillets.

**2** Add wholegrain or German mustard, cream and parsley to create a delicious sauce and stir frequently. Extra cream can be used in this recipe, if you want lots of sauce.

**3** Serve with mashed potato and carrot and zucchini sticks. As an alternative to chicken, use veal, beef or pork strips.

**Serves** 4  **Calories** 192  **Fat** 3.3g  **Preparation** 5 mins  **Cooking** 10 mins

# thai chicken meatballs

**Hint:** This versatile mixture can also be used as meat loaf. You will need to double the mixture. Cook at 356°F/180°C for 1 hour.

**Serves** 4–6 **Calories** 201
**Fat** 0.9g **Preparation** 10 mins
**Cooking** 6 mins

## INGREDIENTS

1 lb/500g chicken breast mince

small bunch chives, finely chopped

½ cup parsley, chopped

½ cup fresh coriander, finely chopped

2 teaspoons Thai seasoning

2cm piece fresh ginger, grated

1 egg

½ cup fresh white breadcrumbs

salt and pepper to taste

1 tablespoon cornstarch

2 tablespoons peanut oil

1 teaspoon sesame oil

## METHOD

**1** Combine all the ingredients except the cornstarch and peanut and sesame oils. Form the mixture into mini meatballs.

**2** Coat the meatballs with the cornstarch and fry in a small amount of peanut oil with a splash of sesame oil for approximately 3 minutes on each side, until cooked through. Serve with rice and sweet chili sauce, for dipping.

# crisp chicken

## INGREDIENTS

1 lb/500g chicken breast fillets, cut into strips

2 tablespoons plain flour

1 egg, beaten

2 tablespoons olive oil

## METHOD

**1** Coat the strips of chicken in the flour first and then the egg.

**2** Heat the olive oil in a frying pan and cook the chicken until golden brown, approximately 3–5 minutes. Serve with a crisp green salad, roasted tomatoes and hot bread rolls.

**Hint:** You can vary this recipe by using fish or pork instead of chicken.

**Serves** 4  **Calories** 107

**Fat** 1.3g  **Preparation** 5 mins

**Cooking** 5 mins

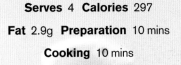

# chicken maryland

**Serves** 4  **Calories** 297
**Fat** 2.9g  **Preparation** 10 mins
**Cooking** 10 mins

## INGREDIENTS

1 lb/500g chicken breast fillets
sprinkle of lemon pepper seasoning
2 tablespoons plain flour
1–2 eggs
dry breadcrumbs
1 tablespoon olive oil
4 slices lean ham
4 slices pineapple
3 oz/80g Cheddar cheese, grated
sprinkle of ground paprika
sprinkle of chives, chopped

## METHOD

**1** Slice the chicken fillets and coat them with lemon pepper seasoning, flour, egg and breadcrumbs.

**2** Heat the olive oil in a frying pan, add the chicken and cook until golden. Top with the ham, pineapple, cheese, ground paprika and chopped chives.

**3** Cover the frying pan and allow the topping to melt. Serve with a crisp green salad and tomato wedges.

# creamy chicken pasta

## INGREDIENTS

1 tablespoon butter

1 lb/500g chicken breast fillets, thinly sliced

1 clove garlic, crushed

small bunch chives, chopped

salt to taste

½ cup fresh parsley, finely chopped

10½ fl oz/300ml cream

sprinkle of pepper

½ lb/250g penne, cooked

## METHOD

**1** Heat half the butter on medium heat in a frying pan. Add the chicken breast fillets, garlic, chopped chives and a little salt.

**2** Cover and cook for 4 minutes, stirring occasionally. Add the remaining butter, parsley, cream, pepper and finally the hot cooked pasta. Stir through to combine. Serve in warmed bowls.

**Serves** 4–6  **Calories** 330

**Fat** 7.5g  **Preparation** 10 mins  **Cooking** 10 mins

**Hint:** This recipe is delicious with thinly sliced chicken breast fillets, but if you don't have time buy a barbecued chicken with all the skin removed. Just combine the meat with a little garlic and butter and proceed according to the recipe. This is a simple but tasty dish that will appeal to all the family.

Fresh garlic and parsley are a must for this dish and remember to cook your pasta to al dente.

# chicken supreme

**Serves** 4 **Calories** 312
**Fat** 5.4g **Preparation** 10 mins
**Cooking** 10 mins

## INGREDIENTS

**2 chicken breast fillets**
**3 oz/80g Cheddar cheese, grated**
**1 bunch fresh asparagus, blanched**
**pepper to taste**
**2 tablespoons plain flour**
**1 egg mixed with 1 tablespoon milk**
**½ cup breadcrumbs to coat**
**a little olive oil**

## METHOD

**1** Slice each chicken breast fillet in half to form a pocket. Fill with cheese, asparagus and a sprinkle of pepper. Close each breast with toothpicks and coat with the flour, egg mixture and breadcrumbs in turn.

**2** Heat the oil in a frying pan and cook the chicken breasts until golden brown. Turn and repeat. Approximately 4–5 minutes on each side is enough. Serve with watercress, asparagus and green beans.

# *sensational*
## *seafood*

# brenda's famous red salmon dip

**Serves** 6 **Calories** 258

**Fat** 2.85g **Preparation** 10 mins

## INGREDIENTS

7⅓ oz/210g canned red salmon

sprinkle of lemon pepper seasoning

sprinkle of ground paprika

½ lb/250g cream cheese

½ bunch chives, chopped

squeeze of fresh lemon juice

## METHOD

**1** Mix all the ingredients together well. Serve with fresh chilled crudités, such as celery, carrots and cauliflower, all cut into bite-sized pieces.

# italian prawns

## INGREDIENTS

1 tablespoon olive oil

1 teaspoon butter

1 small onion, finely chopped

4 cloves garlic, crushed

2 rashers very lean bacon, finely chopped

sprinkle of chili flakes

14 oz/400g canned chopped tomatoes

14 oz/400g green prawns, peeled and deveined

salt and pepper to taste

1 teaspoon ground paprika

pinch of sugar

fresh parsley to garnish

## METHOD

**1** Heat the olive oil and butter in a frying pan. Add the onion, garlic, bacon and chili flakes. Cook until softened, for about 5 minutes.

**2** Add the can of tomatoes, lower the heat and simmer for 30 minutes, uncovered, to reduce the sauce.

**3** Add the prawns and cook only until they change color, turning the heat up to medium. Season to taste and add paprika and sugar. Serve in individual bowls with crusty bread, garnished with parsley, or stir through hot cooked pasta as a main course.

**Serves** 4 **Calories** 91 **Fat** 0.95g **Preparation** 10 mins **Cooking** 40 mins

# whole thai fish

**Serves** 4 **Calories** 615
**Fat** 1.6g **Preparation** 10 mins
**Cooking** 30 mins

## INGREDIENTS

**4 whole fish**

**sprinkle of lemon pepper seasoning**

**1 tablespoon plain flour**

**2 tablespoons olive oil**

**10⅔ oz/300g sweet chili sauce**

**salt and pepper to taste**

## METHOD

**1** Cut or score 3 openings on each side of the fish to allow the flavors to penetrate. Sprinkle with lemon pepper seasoning and coat with the plain flour.

**2** Heat the olive oil in a frying pan. Add the fish (2 at a time) and cook for 5 minutes.

**3** Turn the fish and coat with sweet chili sauce, seasoning while cooking, then cook for a further 8 minutes or until the fish flakes easily. Serve on a bed of jasmine rice, garnished with sliced cucumber, shallots and fresh chopped coriander.

# master soy fish

## INGREDIENTS

1 lb/500g boneless ocean trout fillets

1 tablespoon olive oil

sprinkle of soy sauce

salt and pepper to taste

shallots, chopped to serve

## METHOD

**1** Heat the olive oil in a frying pan. Add the fish fillets and sprinkle a little soy sauce and seasoning on each fillet.

**2** Cover and cook for 2 minutes, turn and repeat.

**3** Serve on a bed of steamed jasmine rice with bok choy, garnished with shallots.

**Hint:** You can use either ocean trout or fresh salmon steak-style cuts as a fool-proof alternative when frying.

**Serves** 4 **Calories** 497
**Fat** 1.6g **Preparation** 5 mins
**Cooking** 5 mins

# saucy smoked fish

**Hint:** To reduce the amount of salt in this dish you may like to soak the smoked fish in water for a short while before cooking.

**Serves** 4 **Calories** 250
**Fat** 2.2g **Preparation** 5 mins
**Cooking** 10 mins

## INGREDIENTS

1 lb/500g smoked fish
2 teaspoons butter
¾ cup milk
¼ teaspoon ground nutmeg
salt and pepper
1 tablespoon plain flour mixed to a paste with 2 tablespoons of milk
¼ cup fresh parsley, chopped

## METHOD

**1** Place the fish in a microwave-safe dish. Add the butter and the milk. Poach the fish in the microwave on medium-high heat for 3–5 minutes or until the fish flakes easily.

**2** Remove the fish from the liquid and set aside. Place nutmeg and salt and pepper in the fish cooking liquid, and stir in the flour and milk mixture.

**3** Reheat the sauce in the microwave on high for 2 minutes, stirring every 30 seconds or until the sauce thickens. Place the fish on plates and spoon over the sauce. Serve with lightly steamed sliced carrots, peas and corn and garnish with parsley.

# seafood soup

### INGREDIENTS

2 medium onions, chopped

2 cloves garlic, chopped

2 teaspoons butter

14 oz/400g canned chopped tomatoes

1 cup fresh, raw seafood such as prawns, fish, oysters and mussels

sprinkle of chili powder

salt and pepper to taste

¼ cup fresh parsley, chopped

small bunch fresh chives, chopped

### METHOD

**1** Soften the onion and garlic in the melted butter in a large saucepan, add the chopped tomatoes and bring to the boil. Simmer for 5 minutes. Add the seafood and simmer for a further 5 minutes.

**2** Add the seasonings, parsley and chives. Serve in warmed bowls with crusty bread.

**Serves** 4  **Calories** 180  **Fat** 1.6g  **Preparation** 10 mins  **Cooking** 10 mins

39

# prawn omelet

**Serves** 4  **Calories** 342
**Fat** 1.8g  **Preparation** 5 mins
**Cooking** 10 mins

## INGREDIENTS

4 large eggs

½ lb/250g cooked shrimp, peeled and deveined

2⅔ oz/75g cabbage, shredded

1 small onion, finely sliced

1 cup bean sprouts

4 shallots, chopped

2 tablespoons water

1 carrot, grated

1 teaspoon olive oil

salt and pepper

## METHOD

**1** Combine all the ingredients except the olive oil and salt and pepper.

**2** Heat the oil in a frying pan.

**3** Pour in the omelet mixture and cook, covered, until set. Cut into 4 portions and turn each portion over. Season to taste. Cover and cook for a further 2 minutes.

# easy
## vegetables

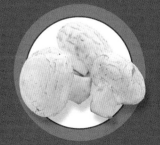

# noodle salad

## INGREDIENTS

10⅔ oz/300g red, savoy or Chinese cabbage, shredded

1 tablespoon soy sauce

1 red capsicum, finely sliced

2 tablespoons honey

4 shallots, chopped

2¼ fl oz/60ml Italian dressing

3½ oz/100g Chinese fried noodles

sprinkle of fresh chili, chopped

½ cup slivered almonds, toasted

## METHOD

**1** Combine all the ingredients and enjoy this fabulous salad.

**Serves** 4–6 **Calories** 259

**Fat** 1.9g **Preparation** 10 mins

# brenda's brilliant rice salad

## INGREDIENTS

1 large onion, chopped

1 cup frozen peas

1 cup frozen corn kernels

2 tablespoons butter

4 cups cooked jasmine rice

4 cloves garlic, crushed

6 large cooked shrimp, peeled and deveined

2 tablespoons olive oil

juice of 1 lemon

3 eggs beaten with 2 tablespoons fresh chives, chopped

sprinkle of mild curry powder

sprinkle of pepper steak seasoning

2 slices lean ham, chopped

¼ cup fresh chives, chopped

## METHOD

**1** Combine the onion, peas and corn and cook in the microwave for 3 minutes in a covered container with 1 tablespoon of the butter. Stir into the cooked jasmine rice.

**2** Melt half of the remaining butter in a frying pan and cook the crushed garlic until soft. Add the prawns to heat through, then add the mixture to the rice with the olive oil and lemon juice.

**3** Place the egg mixture into the frying pan and cook in the remaining butter. When cooked, cut into thin strips and add to the rice, with the mild curry powder and the pepper steak seasoning. Toss to combine, add ham and sprinkle with fresh chives.

**Serves** 4–6 **Calories** 297
**Fat** 4.1g **Preparation** 15 mins
**Cooking** 10 mins

43

# famous mushroom pizza

# famous mushroom pizza

## INGREDIENTS

**base**
1 sachet dry yeast
1 cup warm water
1 teaspoon sugar
3 tablespoons olive oil
1 teaspoon salt
3 cups plain flour, sifted

**topping**
2 tablespoons olive oil
10⅔ oz/300g tomato salsa
1 onion, sliced
2 oz/50g mushrooms, sliced
2 oz/50g Mozzarella cheese, grated
salt and pepper to taste
sprinkle of oregano leaves

## METHOD

**1** Dissolve the yeast in the warm water with the sugar. Let stand until it foams. Add the yeast mixture, olive oil and salt to the flour. Mix to combine and set aside until doubled in size.

**2** Turn out onto a floured board and knead to form a soft dough.

**3** Press a piece of the dough about the size of a tennis ball onto a pizza tray. You could use a cone tray or even a large baking dish.

**4** Preheat the oven to 437°F/225°C. Brush the pizza base with 1 tablespoon of olive oil, spread liberally with salsa, then add the onion and mushrooms. Drizzle with more olive oil and cover liberally with the cheese, salt and pepper to taste. Sprinkle with the oregano leaves. Bake for 20 minutes.

## the girls and the babies

Ten girls and ten babies! We met during our pre-natal classes at the local health clinic. Our first meeting after the birth of our babies was at my place!

This was my second child, but for everyone else it was their first. During our last class, something told me that supporting each other after the big events would be a great idea.

As the big day approached, my thoughts turned to food and to making our first gathering something really special. I wanted my dish to be spectacular! With its pizza base, homemade of course, topped with a tasty tomato salsa, onions, mushrooms and grated cheese and baked to golden perfection in a hot oven – was a real winner!

**Hint:** For the best flavor, use large mushrooms, peeled and thinly sliced. Making your own pizza base is well worth the extra time and effort. Pizza dough can be frozen and used later.

45

# easy vegetables

**Hint:** Use the all-purpose cheese topping as a topping for deli hashbrowns, or mix a little of the topping through scrambled eggs. Alternatively, stuff mushroom caps with the topping and cook in the microwave until the cheese melts. It can also be used as a pizza topping, grilled on muffins or toast, or as a filling for an omelet. Place a little on top of cooked rissoles or chicken or veal schnitzel.

# all-purpose cheese topping

### INGREDIENTS

1 lb/500g Cheddar cheese, grated

sprinkle of ground paprika

small bunch chives, chopped

¼ cup fresh parsley, chopped

sprinkle of pepper

1 red capsicum, finely chopped

**optional ingredients**

bacon, onion and ham, all finely chopped

**Serves** 8 **Calories** 204

**Fat** 5.2g **Preparation** 10 mins

### METHOD

**1** Mix all ingredients together and freeze in a plastic bag or refrigerate until ready to use.

# fresh salsa

### INGREDIENTS

1 baguette, sliced

2 teaspoons garlic bread seasoning

8 tomatoes, finely chopped

1 medium red onion, finely chopped

¼ cup fresh basil, chopped

salt to taste

1 tablespoon olive oil

1 fl oz/30ml balsamic vinegar

**Serves** 8 **Calories** 98 **Fat** 1g

**Preparation** 10 mins

### METHOD

**1** In a bowl, combine all ingredients, except for the bread.

**2** Spread sliced crusty bread with butter and a sprinkle of garlic bread seasoning. Grill or bake until golden brown.

**3** Serve the fresh salsa on hot garlic bread. This salsa is good if prepared a few hours in advance.

# *extravagent*
# *eggs*

# extravagent eggs

**Hint:** Using a sharp knife, cut a small piece of ham. Don't cut through the ham – rather, try to create a small area to hold in the egg.

**Hint:** Finely chop ingredients such as capsicum, mushrooms, shallots or cabbage before incorporating into the omelet mixture. Also grate the cheese. It will help to disperse all of the flavors.

## easy ham and eggs

### INGREDIENTS

1 thick slice ham

1 egg

¾ oz /25g Cheddar cheese, grated

sprinkle of ground paprika

¼ cup fresh parsley, chopped

small bunch chives, chopped

**Serves** 1 **Calories** 214

**Fat** 3.5g **Preparation** 5 mins

**Cooking** 2 mins

### METHOD

**1** Place a sheet of baking parchment on a saucer. On top of this put the ham slice and break the egg onto it. Try to maneuver the yolk to the middle of the ham and have the egg white cover the rest until it partially flows over the edge.

**2** The rounded base of the saucer will help hold the shape of the egg. Pierce the yolk and sprinkle a little grated cheese onto the egg, then sprinkle with paprika, parsley and chives.

**3** Cover the saucer, put into a microwave and cook on high for 1½ minutes or until the egg is the way you like it.

## easy perfect omelet

### INGREDIENTS

4 large eggs

1 tablespoon thickened cream

¾ cup all-purpose cheese topping (page 46)

1 tablespoon olive oil

salt and pepper to taste

### METHOD

**1** Gently beat together all the ingredients in a small bowl.

**2** Heat the oil in a frying pan. Pour the egg mixture into a frying pan, cover, and cook on full power until set. This will take about 5 minutes. To turn the omelet, take two corners of the baking parchment and pull to one side and your omelet will fold in half perfectly. Serve with a little rocket.

**Serves** 2 **Calories** 268.5 **Fat** 13g **Preparation** 5 mins **Cooking** 5 mins

easy perfect omelet

# toad in the hole

**Serves** 4  **Calories** 148
**Fat** 2.9g  **Preparation** 5 mins
**Cooking** 5 mins

## INGREDIENTS

a little soft butter

4 slices bread, with a
hole the size of a large coin
piece cut out of the center

4 eggs

salt and pepper to taste

¼ cup fresh chives, chopped

## METHOD

**1** Butter the bread and place buttered side down in a heated frying pan. Cook until golden brown.

**2** Turn over and break an egg into the hole in each slice of bread. Season with pepper and salt to taste, cover and cook until the egg is set. Sprinkle with a little chopped fresh chives before serving. Turn again for a well done egg.

# *delicious desserts*

# delicious desserts

**Hint:** Store left over fruit in a plastic bag to prevent it discoloring.

# granny's apple pancakes

## INGREDIENTS

4 Granny Smith apples, peeled and thinly sliced
2 tablespoons butter
2 tablespoons brown sugar
sprinkle of mixed spice
½ cup sultanas
13 oz/375g pancake mix
icing sugar

Serves 6  Calories 279
Fat 2.8g  Preparation 5 mins
Cooking 10 mins

## METHOD

**1** In a frying pan, sauté thinly sliced apples in butter and brown sugar until soft. Add a sprinkle of mixed spice and sultanas.

**2** Pour pancake mix over the fruit. Place the lid on the pan and cook until firm. Sprinkle with icing sugar, cut into slices and serve with ice cream, custard or cream. Serve upside-down to display the beautiful glazed fruit.

**Hint:** For extra flavor, add fresh passionfruit after cooking.

# rhubarb and apple

## INGREDIENTS

1 bunch rhubarb, stems only, washed and chopped
2 Granny Smith apples, peeled and sliced
½ cup sugar
¾ cup water
sprinkle of ground nutmeg

## METHOD

**1** Place the rhubarb and apples into a large microwave-safe bowl. Add the sugar and water.

**2** Cook, uncovered, in a microwave on high for 15 minutes, stirring every 5 minutes.

**3** Sprinkle a little ground nutmeg over the fruit mixture. Serve with cream, custard or ice cream.

Serves 4  Calories 155  Fat 0.1g  Preparation 10 mins  Cooking 15 mins

# rhubarb and apple

# fruity pan scones

## INGREDIENTS

1 cup sultanas

3 cups self-raising flour, sifted

1 cup milk

1 cup thickened cream

a little extra flour

## METHOD

**1** Preheat an over to 437°F/225°c. Add the sultanas to the flour, then add the milk and cream. Using a knife, stir to make a sticky dough.

**2** Turn the mixture out onto a floured board, sprinkle with a little extra flour and pat into a rectangular shape, approximately 3cm high.

**3** Cut out the scones with a scone cutter. Cook the scones in the oven for 15 minutes.

**Serves** 6  **Calories** 416

**Fat** 5.4g  **Preparation** 5 mins

**Cooking** 17 mins

# fabulous fruit salad

## INGREDIENTS

1 peach

1 green apple

1 red apple

1 mango

a few slices rockmelon

1 punnet strawberries

generous sprinkle of mint flakes

13 oz/375g canned pineapple pieces with juice

sugar to taste

## METHOD

**1** Dice all the fruit ingredients except the pineapple, and gently mix together in a bowl.

**2** Add the mint flakes and the pineapple pieces with juice. Gently stir through.

**3** Dust the fruit salad lightly with sugar. Refrigerate until cool.

**Serves** 4 **Calories** 78.6g

**Fat** 0.1g **Preparation** 5 mins

# banana surprise

**Serves** 4  **Calories** 202

**Fat** 3.8g  **Preparation** 5 mins

**Cooking** 1 min

## INGREDIENTS

**2 tablespoons honey**

**2 tablespoons butter**

**sprinkle of ground nutmeg**

**2 firm bananas, sliced into chunks**

**sprinkle of ground cinnamon**

## METHOD

**1** Place the honey and butter into a microwave-safe container. Sprinkle the ground nutmeg over the top and heat in a microwave for 30 seconds on high.

**2** Gently stir the bananas through the warm honey mixture and cook on high for 30 seconds to warm. Sprinkle with a little ground cinnamon. Serve with ice cream, cream or sour cream.

# banana pancakes

## INGREDIENTS

2 tablespoons butter

2 cups pancake mix

2 medium bananas, sliced

¼ cup cinnamon sugar

1⅓ cups golden syrup

6 small scoop ice cream

## METHOD

**1** Combine the pancake batter and sliced bananas.

**2** Heat the butter in a frying pan and cook the pancake mixture in butter in the pan until bubbles appear on the surface. Turn and cook until golden in color.

**3** Serve each portion with a good sprinkle of cinnamon sugar, golden syrup, and a scoop of ice cream.

**Serves** 6  **Calories** 257
**Fat** 9.2g  **Preparation** 5 mins
**Cooking** 6 mins

**Hint:** This cake cuts well if prepared the day before it is required.

# forest berry magic

## INGREDIENTS

1 good quality chocolate cake mix

small quantity of liqueur, optional

1 punnet fresh strawberries, or other berries in season

26½ oz/750ml cream, whipped

dark chocolate, grated

## METHOD

**1** Prepare the cake mix, using a fork to mix the ingredients, but do not over-beat.

**2** Cut out three circles of baking parchment the size of a dinner plate and place each circle onto a plate.

**3** Put a third of the cake mix onto each plate circle and cook each individually on high in the microwave for 3–4 minutes. Allow to cool.

**4** Select one cake, invert it, and remove the baking paper. Sprinkle with liqueur if desired, and top with some the fruit and whipped cream.

**5** Place the second cake on top of the first, and repeat. Finally, add the third layer, then cover the entire cake with the remaining cream. Top with a little fruit and the grated dark chocolate.

**6** Place a large bowl over the cake and refrigerate overnight. Make sure the bowl does not touch the cake top.

**Serves** 6–8 **Calories** 324

**Fat** 10.5g **Preparation** 5 mins

**Cooking** 10 mins

# blueberry soft-bake cookies

## INGREDIENTS

5⅓ oz/150g plain flour

1½ teaspoons baking powder

½ teaspoon cinnamon

2 oz/55g butter, cubed,
plus extra for greasing

3 oz/85g caster sugar

3½ fl oz/100ml milk

5⅓ oz/150g fresh blueberries

## METHOD

**1** Preheat the oven to 374°F/190°C. Grease a large baking tray. Sift the flour, baking powder and cinnamon into a bowl. Rub in the butter, using your fingertips, until the mixture resembles breadcrumbs, then stir in the sugar.

**2** Stir in the milk and blueberries until just combined – the dough should be sticky. Spoon 8 mounds, spaced well apart, onto the baking tray and cook for 20 minutes or until golden. Cool on a wire rack for a few minutes before serving.

**Hint:** If you fancy a change, try using a few chopped strawberries instead of the blueberries. You can also substitute your favorite chocolate for some of the berry quantity. My boys love these made with two-thirds blueberry and one-third white chocolate. These are a delicious muffin-type cookie and are best eaten hot.

**Serves** 4 **Calories** 313

**Fat** 9.6g **Preparation** 10 mins

**Cooking** 20 mins

# basic tomato sauce

### INGREDIENTS

2 cloves garlic, crushed

2 tablespoons olive oil

14 oz/400g chopped tomatoes

10 leaves fresh basil, chopped

sprinkle of sea salt

sprinkle of cracked black peppercorns

### METHOD

**1** Gently fry the crushed garlic in the olive oil until it softens. Add the rest of the ingredients and simmer, uncovered, until reduced to half the quantity. Serve with freshly cooked pasta, vegetarian lasagne, cooked crumbed meat, fish or chicken. Top with grated Cheddar cheese and grill until golden brown.

**Serves** 4 **Calories** 354 **Fat** 3.8g **Preparation** 5 mins **Cooking** 10 mins

# curry mayonnaise

### INGREDIENTS

½ cup whole-egg mayonnaise

¼ cup fresh parsley, finely chopped

½ teaspoon curry powder

squeeze of fresh lime juice

### METHOD

**1** Mix all ingredients together. Serve with poached salmon, steamed chicken breast, cooked prawns on a bed of rocket and Mesclun salad, fresh oysters, pasta with smoked salmon or Danish open sandwiches of chicken or salmon.

**Serves** 4 **Calories** 470 **Fat** 5.8g **Preparation** 5 mins

# mushroom sauce

### INGREDIENTS

2 teaspoons butter

1 clove garlic, crushed

½ lb/250g flat mushrooms, chopped

salt and pepper to taste

2 teaspoons plain flour

small bunch chives, chopped

3 tablespoons skim milk

### METHOD

**1** Heat the butter in a frying pan over a medium heat, add the garlic, mushrooms, salt and pepper.

**2** Cover and cook for a few minutes until the mushrooms soften but are still firm. Sprinkle the flour over the mushrooms and blend with a fork, then add the chives. Blend in the milk to create a smooth sauce. Reduce heat and simmer for 1–2 minutes.

**3** Serve on hot toasted sourdough bread or crusty bread.

**Serves** 4 **Calories** 165 **Fat** 5g **Preparation** 5 mins **Cooking** 5 mins

# glossary

**al dente:** an Italian cooking term for ingredients that are cooked until tender but still firm to the bite; usually applied to pasta.

**balsamic vinegar:** a mild, extremely fragrant, wine-based vinegar made in northern Italy. Traditionally, the vinegar is aged for at least 7 years in a series of casks made of various woods.

**baste:** to moisten food while it is cooking by spooning or brushing on liquid or fat.

**bain marie:** a saucepan standing in a large pan which is filled with boiling water to keep liquids at simmering point. A double boiler will do the same job.

**beat:** to stir thoroughly and vigorously.

**blanch:** to plunge into boiling water and then, in some cases, into cold water. Fruits and nuts are blanched to remove skin easily.

**blend:** to mix thoroughly.

**brown:** to cook in a small amount of fat until brown.

**butter:** to spread with softened or melted butter.

**butterfly:** to slit a piece of food in half horizontally, cutting it almost through so that when opened it resembles butterfly wings. Chops, large prawns and thick fish fillets are often butterflied so that they cook more quickly.

**caramelize:** to melt sugar until it is a golden-brown syrup.

**champignons:** small mushrooms, usually canned.

**coat:** to cover with a thin layer of flour, sugar, nuts, crumbs, poppy or sesame seeds, cinnamon sugar or a few of the ground spices.

**cream:** to make soft, smooth and creamy by rubbing with back of spoon or by beating with a mixer. Usually applied to fat and sugar.

**croutons:** small toasted or fried cubes of bread.

**crudités:** raw vegetables, whether cut in slices or sticks to nibble plain or with a dipping sauce, or shredded and tossed as salad with a simple dressing.

**cube:** to cut into small pieces with six equal sides.

**curdle:** to cause milk or sauce to separate into solid and liquid. An example, overcooked egg mixtures.

**deglaze:** to dissolve congealed cooking juices or glaze on the bottom of a pan by adding a liquid, then scraping and stirring vigorously whilst bringing the liquid to the boil. Juices may be used to make gravy or to add to sauce.

**devilled:** a dish or sauce that is highly seasoned with a hot ingredient such as mustard, worcestershire sauce or cayenne pepper.

**dice:** to cut into small cubes.

**dietary fiber:** a plant-cell material that is undigested or only partially digested in the human body but which promotes healthy digestion of other food matter.

**dissolve:** mix a dry ingredient with liquid until absorbed.

**drizzle:** to pour in a fine thread-like stream over a surface.

**dust:** to sprinkle or coat lightly with flour or icing sugar.

**entrée:** in Europe, the 'entry' or hors d'oeuvre; in North America, the main course.

**fillet:** a special cut of beef, lamb, pork or veal; breast of poultry and game; fish cut off the bone lengthwise.

**flake:** to break into small pieces with a fork.

**flame:** to ignite warmed alcohol over food.

**fold in:** a gentle, careful combining of a light or delicate mixture with a heavier mixture using a metal spoon.

**garnish:** to decorate food, usually with something edible.

**glaze:** a thin coating of beaten egg, syrup or aspic which is brushed over pastry, fruits or cooked meats.

**gratin:** a dish cooked in the oven or under the grill so that it develops a brown crust. Breadcrumbs or cheese may be sprinkled on top first. Shallow gratin dishes ensure a maximum area of crust.

**grease:** to rub or brush lightly with oil or fat.

**joint:** to cut poultry, game or small animals into serving pieces by dividing at the joint.

**julienne:** to cut food into match-like strips.

**knead:** to work dough using the heel of the hand with a pressing motion, while stretching and folding the dough.

**line:** to cover the inside of a container with paper, to protect or aid in removing mixture.

**marinade:** a seasoned liquid, usually an oil and acid mixture, in which meats or other foods are soaked to soften and give more flavor.

**marinate:** to let food stand in a marinade to season and tenderize.

**melt:** to heat until liquified.

**mince:** to grind into very small pieces.

**mix:** to combine ingredients by stirring.

**olive oil:** various grades of oil extract from olives. Extra virgin olive oil has a full, fruity flavor and the lowest acidity. Virgin olive oil is slightly higher in acidity and lighter in flavor. Pure olive oil is a processed blend of olive oils and has the highest acidity and lightest taste.

**peel:** to strip away outside covering.

**poach:** to simmer gently in enough hot liquid to cover, using care to retain shape of food.

**purée:** a smooth paste, usually of vegetables or fruits, made by putting foods through a sieve, food mill or liquefying in a blender or food processor.

**reduce:** to cook over a very high heat, uncovered, until the liquid is reduced by evaporation.

**rubbing-in:** a method of incorporating fat into flour, by use of fingertips only. Also incorporates air into mixture.

**salsa:** a juice derived from the main ingredient being cooked or a sauce added to a dish to enhance its flavor. In Italy the term is often used for pasta sauces; in Mexico the name usually applies to uncooked sauces served as an accompaniment, especially to corn chips.

**sauté:** to cook or brown in small amount of hot fat.

**score:** to mark food with cuts, notches of lines to prevent curling or to make food more attractive.

**scald:** to bring just to boiling point, usually for milk. Also to rinse with boiling water.

**sear:** to brown the surface quickly over high heat.

**seasoned flour:** flour with salt and pepper added.

**sift:** to shake a dry, powdered substance through a sieve or sifter to remove any lumps and give lightness.

**simmer:** to cook food gently in liquid that bubbles steadily just below boiling point so that the food cooks in even heat without breaking up.

**skim:** to remove a surface layer (often of impurities and scum) from a liquid with a metal spoon or small ladle.

**slivered:** sliced in long, thin pieces. Usually refers to nuts, especially almonds.

**stir-fry:** to cook thin slices of meat and vegetable over a high heat in a small amount of oil, stirring constantly cook evenly in a short time. Traditionally done in a wok; however, a heavy based frying pan may be used.

**stock:** a liquid containing flavors, extracts and nutrients of bones, meat, fish or vegetables.

**thicken:** to thicken a hot liquid by stirring a thin, smooth paste of arrowroot, cornstarch or flour with an equal amount of cold water until thickened.

**toss:** to gently mix ingredients with two forks or a fork and spoon.

**whip:** to beat rapidly, incorporate air and produce expansion.

**zest:** thin outer layer of citrus fruits containing the aromatic citrus oil. It is usually thinly pared with a vegetable peeler or grated with a zester or grater to separate it from the bitter white pith underneath.

61

# weights and *measures*

Cooking is not an exact science: one does not require finely calibrated scales, pipettes and scientific equipment to cook, yet the conversion to metric measures in some countries and its interpretations must have intimidated many a good cook.

Weights are given in the recipes only for ingredients such as meats, fish, poultry and some vegetables. Remember, however, that a few grams/ounces one way or the other will not affect the success of your dish.

Although recipes have been tested using the Australian Standard 250ml cup, 20ml tablespoon and 5ml teaspoon, they will work just as well with the US and Canadian 8fl oz cup, or the UK 300ml cup. We have used graduated cup measures in preference to tablespoon measures so that proportions are always the same. Where tablespoon measures have been given, these are not crucial measures, so using the smaller tablespoon of the US or UK will not affect the recipe's success. At least we all agree on the teaspoon size.

For breads, cakes and pastries, the only area which might cause concern is where eggs are used, as proportions will then vary. If working with a 250ml or 300ml cup, use large eggs (65g/2$^{1}$/4 oz), adding a little more liquid to the recipe for 300ml cup measures if it seems necessary. Use the medium-sized eggs (55g/2 oz) with 8fl oz cup measure. A graduated set of measuring cups and spoons is recommended, the cups in particular for measuring dry ingredients. Remember to level such ingredients to ensure their accuracy.

### English Measures
All measurements are similar to Australian with two exceptions: the English cup measures 300ml/10fl oz, whereas the Australian cup measures 250ml/8$^{3}$/4fl oz. The English tablespoon (the Australian dessertspoon) measures 14.8ml/$^{1}$/2 fl oz against the Australian tablespoon of 20ml/$^{2}$/3 fl oz.

The Imperial measurement is 20fl oz to the pint, 40fl oz a quart and 160fl oz one gallon.

### American Measures
The American reputed pint is 16fl oz, a quart is equal to 32fl oz, the American gallon, 128fl oz. The American tablespoon is equal to 14.8mL/$^{1}$/2 fl oz, and the teaspoon is 5mL/$^{1}$/6 fl oz. The cup measure is 250mL/8$^{3}$/4fl oz.

### Dry Measures
All the measures are level, so when you have filled a cup or spoon, level it off with the edge of a knife. The scale opposite is the 'cook's equivalent'; it is not an exact conversion of metric to imperial measurement. To calculate the exact metric equivalent yourself, multiply ounces by 28.349523 to obtain grams, or divide grams by 28.349523 to obtain ounces.

| Metric | Imperial |
|---|---|
| g = grams | oz = ounces |
| kg = kilograms | lb = pounds |
| 15g | $^{1}$/2oz |
| 20g | $^{2}$/3oz |
| 30g | 1oz |
| 55g | 2oz |
| 85g | 3oz |
| 115g | 4oz/$^{1}$/4 lb |
| 145g | 5oz |
| 170g | 6oz |
| 200g | 7oz |
| 225g | 8oz/$^{1}$/2 lb |
| 255g | 9oz |
| 285g | 10oz |
| 310g | 11oz |
| 340g | 12oz/$^{3}$/4 lb |
| 370g | 13oz |
| 400g | 14oz |
| 425g | 15oz |
| 1kg | 1lb/35.2oz/2.2 lb |
| 1.5kg | 3.3 lb |

# weights and measures

## Oven Temperatures

The Celsius temperatures given here are not exact; they have been rounded off and are given as a guide only. Follow the manufacturer's temperature guide, relating it to oven description given in the recipe. Remember gas ovens are hottest at the top, electric ovens at the bottom and convection-fan forced ovens are usually even throughout. We included Regulo numbers for gas cookers, which may assist. To convert °C to °F multiply °C by 9, divide by 5, then add 32.

## Oven Temperatures

|  | C° | F° | Regular |
|---|---|---|---|
| Very slow | 120 | 250 | 1 |
| Slow | 150 | 300 | 2 |
| Moderately slow | 160 | 325 | 3 |
| Moderate | 180 | 350 | 4 |
| Moderately hot | 190–200 | 370–400 | 5–6 |
| Hot | 210–220 | 410–440 | 6–7 |
| Very hot | 230 | 450 | 8 |
| Super hot | 250–290 | 475–500 | 9–10 |

## Cake Dish Sizes

| Metric | Imperial |
|---|---|
| 15cm | 6in |
| 18cm | 7in |
| 20cm | 8in |
| 23cm | 9in |

## Loaf Dish Sizes

| Metric | Imperial |
|---|---|
| 23x12cm | 9x5in |
| 25x8cm | 10x3in |
| 28x18cm | 11x7in |

## Liquid Measures

| Metric millilitres | Imperial fluid ounce | Cup and Spoon |
|---|---|---|
| 5mL | 1/6 fl oz | 1 teaspoon |
| 14.8mL | 1/2 fl oz | 1 dessertspoon |
| 20mL | 2/3 fl oz | 1 tablespoon |
| 30mL | 1 fl oz | (1 tablespoon plus 2 teaspoons) |

| | | |
|---|---|---|
| 55ml | 2fl oz | |
| 62ml | 2 1/6 fl oz | 1/4 cup |
| 85ml | 3fl oz | 1/3 cup |
| 115ml | 4fl oz | |
| 125ml | 4 1/2 fl oz | 1/2 cup |
| 150ml | 5 1/4 fl oz | |
| 185ml | 6 1/2 fl oz | 3/4 cup |
| 225ml | 8fl oz | |
| 250ml | 8 3/4 fl oz | 1 cup |
| 285ml | 10fl oz | |
| 340ml | 12fl oz | |
| 375ml | 13fl oz | 1 1/2 cups |
| 400ml | 14fl oz | |
| 435ml | 15 1/3 fl oz | 1 3/4 cups |
| 455ml | 16fl oz | |
| 500ml | 17 1/2 fl oz | 2 cups |
| 567ml | 20fl oz | 1 pint |
| 625ml | 22fl oz | 2 1/2 cups |
| 1 litre | 35fl oz | 4 cups |

## Cup Measurements

One cup is equal to the following weights.

| | Metric | Imperial |
|---|---|---|
| Almonds, flaked | 90g | 3oz |
| Almonds, slivered, ground | 115g | 4oz |
| Almonds, kernel | 145g | 5oz |
| Apples, dried, chopped | 115g | 4oz |
| Apricots, dried, chopped | 170g | 6oz |
| Breadcrumbs, packet | 115g | 4oz |
| Breadcrumbs, soft | 55g | 2oz |
| Cheese, grated | 115g | 4oz |
| Choc bits | 145g | 5oz |
| Coconut, desiccated | 85g | 3oz |
| Cornflakes | 30g | 1oz |
| Currants | 145g | 5oz |
| Flour | 115g | 4oz |
| Fruit, dried (mixed, sultanas etc) | 170g | 6oz |
| Ginger, crystallised, glace | 225g | 8oz |
| Honey, treacle, Golden syrup | 285g | 10oz |
| Mixed peel | 200g | 7oz |
| Nuts, chopped | 115g | 4oz |
| Prunes, chopped | 200g | 7oz |
| Rice, cooked | 145g | 5oz |
| Rice, uncooked | 200g | 7oz |
| Rolled oats | 85g | 3oz |
| Sesame seeds | 115g | 4oz |
| Shortening (butter, margarine) | 225g | 8oz |
| Sugar, brown | 145g | 5oz |
| Sugar, granulated or caster | 225g | 8oz |
| Sugar, sifted icing | 145g | 5oz |
| Wheatgerm | 55g | 2oz |

## Length

Some of us still have trouble converting imperial length to metric. In this scale, measures have been rounded off to the easiest to use and most acceptable figures. To obtain the exact metric equivalent in converting inches to centimeters, multiply inches by 2.54 whereby 1 inch equals 25.4 millimeters and 1 millimeter equals 0.03937 inches.

mm = millimeters    in = inches
cm = centimeters    ft = feet

| | |
|---|---|
| 5mm, 0.5cm | 1/4 in |
| 10mm, 1.0cm | 1/2 in |
| 20mm, 2.0cm | 3/4 in |
| 2 1/2 cm | 1in |
| 5cm | 2in |
| 7 1/2 cm | 3in |
| 10cm | 4in |
| 12 1/2 cm | 5in |
| 15cm | 6in |
| 18cm | 7in |
| 20cm | 8in |
| 23cm | 9in |
| 25cm | 10in |
| 28cm | 11in |
| 30cm | 12in (1ft) |

# index